Pictures
at an
Exhibition

Anna Harwell Celenza

Illustrated by
JoAnn E. Kitchel

ini Charlesbridge

First paperback edition 2005

Published by Charlesbridge
85 Main Street, Watertown, MA 02472
(617) 926-0329
www.charlesbridge.com

Library of Congress Cataloging-in-Publication Data
Celenza, Anna Harwell.
Pictures at an exhibition/Anna Harwell Celenza; illustrated by JoAnn E. Kitchel.
p.   cm.
One computer optical disk (digital; 4 ¾") in jacket pocket.
Summary: Suggests how the death of a friend, Victor Hartmann,
inspired the music of Modest Mussorgsky in St. Petersburg in the 1870s.
ISBN-13: 978-1-57091-492-8; ISBN-10: 1-57091-492-3 (reinforced for library use)
ISBN-13: 978-1-57091-686-1; ISBN-10: 1-57091-686-1 (softcover)
[1. Mussorgsky, Modest Petrovich, 1839-1881—Juvenile fiction.
2. Mussorgsky, Modest Petrovich, 1839-1881—Fiction. 3. Composers—Fiction.
4. Russia—History—1801-1917—Fiction.] I. Kitchel, JoAnn E., ill. II. Title.
PZ7.C314   Pi 2003
[Fic]—dc21   2002002331

Printed in Korea
(hc) 10 9 8 7 6 5
(sc) 10 9 8 7 6 5 4 3 2 1

Illustrations done in watercolor and ink on Arches cold press paper
Display type and text type set in Giovanni and Della Robbia
Color separations by Sung In Printing
Printed and bound February 2010 by Sung In Printing in Gunpo-Si, Kyonggi-Do, Korea
Production supervision by Brian G. Walker
Designed by Diane M. Earley

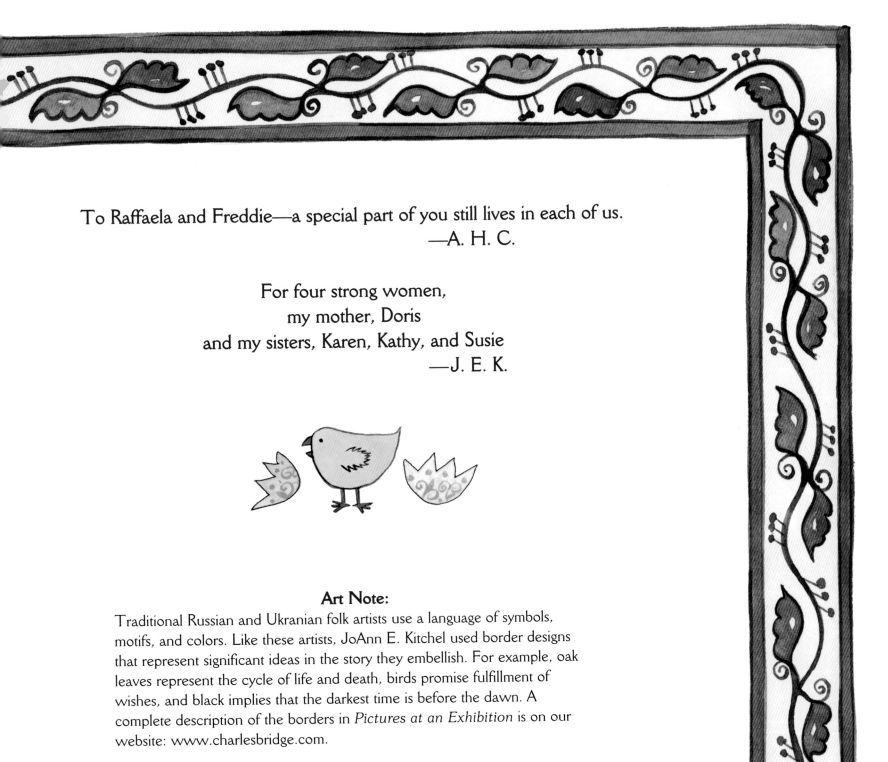

To Raffaela and Freddie—a special part of you still lives in each of us.
—A. H. C.

For four strong women,
my mother, Doris
and my sisters, Karen, Kathy, and Susie
—J. E. K.

Art Note:

Traditional Russian and Ukranian folk artists use a language of symbols, motifs, and colors. Like these artists, JoAnn E. Kitchel used border designs that represent significant ideas in the story they embellish. For example, oak leaves represent the cycle of life and death, birds promise fulfillment of wishes, and black implies that the darkest time is before the dawn. A complete description of the borders in *Pictures at an Exhibition* is on our website: www.charlesbridge.com.

St. Petersburg was a vibrant, bustling city in the 1870s. Business was booming. People took pride in their Russian heritage. It was an exciting time, full of hope and prosperity. Everyone looked to the future with great expectations . . . especially the city's young artists and musicians. After centuries of exclusion, Russia had finally been embraced by the rest of Europe. Russian culture was all the rage.

"It's finally finished!" cried Victor as he burst through the front door.

Modest and Vladimir looked up from the piano. They were playing through a scene from Modest's new opera.

"What are you talking about?" asked Vladimir.

"My designs for the building competition," said Victor. "You know, for the City Gate in Kiev." He pushed the breakfast dishes to one side and carefully spread his drawing out on the table. "Come have a look!" he said. "You'll love it!"

Vladimir chuckled as he got up from his chair, "No one can accuse you of false modesty, Victor."

Modest nudged Vladimir. "Stop teasing him," he said. "You're the same way when you finish writing one of your articles." He walked over to the table and studied his friend's drawing. "It's fantastic, Victor! The judges would be fools not to choose your design."

"I agree," said Vladimir. "It's magnificent!"

"Do you really think so?" asked Victor. "Oh, I hope you're right. It would be a dream come true to finally see one of my designs built in stone."

Such was the scene on a sunny March morning in 1873. Modest Mussorgsky, Victor Hartmann, and Vladimir Stasov were spending the day as they did most days, working together on various projects. They belonged to a group of young artists and musicians trying to make their mark in the world. All three had great plans for the future. Modest wanted to write operas celebrating the glory of the Russian people. Victor dreamed of decorating his homeland with fantastic towers and gates. And Vladimir hoped to travel far and wide, telling the world about Russia's great talents.

But life does not always go as planned, and on July 23, 1873, the lives of these three friends took a turn for the worse.

"No!" cried Modest. "Victor can't be dead! I saw him just last week."

"It was quite unexpected," said Vladimir, his voice cracking with sorrow. "A blood vessel burst near his heart."

Modest's face turned ashen white. "It's all my fault," he said. He walked across the room and slumped down in a chair.

"Don't blame yourself," said Vladimir. "There was nothing you could have done."

Modest buried his face in his hands. "You're wrong," he cried. "Victor was complaining of a headache last week, but I wouldn't listen. I wanted him to carry some boxes over to the theater for me. When he refused, I got angry. I called him lazy and said he was faking the headache." Modest took a bottle from the table next to him and smashed it against the wall. "Why didn't I listen to him?"

Vladimir tried to comfort his friend, but Modest pushed him away. "I don't want to talk to anyone," he said. "Just leave me alone."

For the next few weeks, no one saw much of Modest. He hid himself away from friends, suffering the loss of dear Victor in solitude. When Modest finally did appear, he wasn't the same man. His face was swollen. His hands shook. He was irritable and mean. Modest had stopped writing music, and his friends were worried.

"What are we going to do about Modest?" asked Alexander, a young composer. "I approached him on the street yesterday, but he wouldn't even look at me."

"It hurts to see Modest suffering like this," said Vladimir. "But there isn't much we can do right now. I'm trying to organize an exhibition of Victor's art. If I can pull it off, perhaps that will help."

"Yes!" said Mikhail, another friend. "Seeing Victor's art again might just do the trick. If you want help, I'll do everything I can."

"Me too," said Alexander. "Just tell me what you need."

So Vladimir and the others set to work gathering Victor's art. By February they had put together a huge exhibition with over 400 paintings and drawings. On the day of the opening, Vladimir visited Modest and invited him to come.

"No!" yelled Modest. "I'm not interested. Victor is dead, and I want nothing more to do with him. Do you understand?"

"I understand," said Vladimir calmly. He closed the door, locked it, and slid the key into his pocket.

"What do you think you're doing?" cried Modest.

"I won't take 'no' for an answer," said Vladimir. "Either you agree to come to the exhibition with me now, or you get used to the idea of a roommate."

Modest narrowed his eyes and sneered, "Have you considered joining the army, Vladimir? You're very good at telling people what to do. I'm sure they would make you a general."

Vladimir crossed his arms and leaned against the door. "I'm still waiting for an answer," he said.

Modest threw his hands in the air. "Alright. You win. I'll come with you. Just let me get my coat."

When they reached the gallery, Vladimir put his arm around his friend's shoulders and said, "A special part of Victor still lives in each of us, Modest. Don't shut him out. Remember Victor, and the pain of his passing will ease."

"If I have to do this, then at least let me do it alone," replied Modest. He pulled away from Vladimir, opened the door to the gallery, and grudgingly stepped inside. Modest stood dumbfounded. Every inch was filled with Victor's hopes and dreams, his fears, and his greatest triumphs. Modest looked across the room and spotted a familiar face—a gnarled little gnome Victor had drawn several years ago. Slowly, he made his way toward the drawing. He stared into the gnome's anxious eyes. "I know just how you feel," he whispered.

As he wandered through the gallery, each picture sparked a memory. There was a gloomy castle made for one of Mikhail's operas, and designs for some canary costumes used in a ballet. The next painting showed a park in Paris. Lovers strolled beneath the trees while children squabbled next to a swing. "That carefree day was so long ago," Modest thought to himself.

There were many portraits in the exhibition, faces both familiar and strange. The wealthy Samuel Goldenberg with his fur hat and arrogant sneer. And Schmuÿl, the old beggar, crying in the street. There was a painting of the weary peasants Victor and Modest had seen on the roadway last year, lumbering through the mud with their oxen. Victor's whole life was alive on canvas. From the early-morning bustle of the marketplace to the still, dark shadows of candle-lit catacombs. Even Baba-Yaga the witch was there, from Victor's favorite fairy tale, sitting in her hut built on chicken legs.

Each picture was special, but one picture in particular, "The Great Gate of Kiev," stirred Modest's soul. "Oh Victor," he sighed, "This was to be your greatest achievement—a glorious monument to heroic Russia and almighty God!" Modest's eyes filled with tears. "Now it will never be more than a dream. If only I could build it for you." Modest stood in front of the drawing for a long time. He studied the delicate windows of the church and imagined the stone walls rising heroically toward heaven. Suddenly, a smile spread across his lips. "Maybe I *can* build it for you!" he thought. Modest rushed from the gallery. "Thank you, General!" he cried out happily behind him.

Modest went straight to his piano. He hadn't played a note in months, but suddenly his heart was full of music. Modest thought about Victor's art, and one by one the spirit of each picture filled the room. The anxious gnome appeared first. He scampered up out of the piano and scurried around the room in a feverish dance, then stealthily crept along the floor before running away.

Next, mist rose from the piano and an ancient castle appeared. A lone troubadour sat at the gate, singing a slow, sad song from ages past. Modest listened for a while, but then his mind began to wander to another part of the exhibition. A ray of sun broke through the mist, and the castle was transformed into a beautiful park, full of birds and jeering children. "NYAA na. NYAA na," they cried as they chased one another around a tree.

Modest laughed at their sing-song jeers. In an instant, they were gone—replaced by plodding oxen, straining under the weight of a heavy load.

"Peep, peep," chirped the canary chicks. As Modest played, they hopped out of the piano and scampered across the room. "Peep, peep." Fluttering and pecking, they tried desperately to break free from their shells.

Mr. Goldenberg was not amused. He stepped out of the piano and looked about the room with an arrogant sneer on his face. Obviously dissatisfied, he slowly walked across the room and out the door, ignoring poor Schmuÿl, who stood whimpering in the corner.

The market women scurried past next, whispering gossip on their way into town. They didn't seem to hear the mournful tones that rose from the dark catacombs beneath the street. But Baba-Yaga heard them. The song of death was music to her ears. She leapt from the piano in her monstrous hut and thrashed about frantically, looking for children to terrify.

Growing in strength and emotion, each picture filled the room with music, as a special part of Victor came to life. "Now we shall build your Great Gate of Kiev!" cried Modest. He lifted his hands slowly and then slammed them down on the keyboard over and over. Mighty chords rose majestically toward heaven in a hymn of thanks—heroic Russia and the glory of God combined!

For many weeks Modest worked at his piano, blending the musical pictures into a special composition. He even added a picture of himself, walking through the gallery, from one painting to the next. When the composition was finally finished, he closed the music and carefully wrote the title across the front page: *Pictures at an Exhibition.* He slid the music into an envelope and sent it to Vladimir with the following inscription:

To the Great General,
Sponsor of the
Hartmann Exhibition,
in memory of dear Victor.
June 27, 1874

In the years that followed, Modest returned to his operas and friends. With Victor alive in him, he followed his dreams with great success.

Vladimir also followed his dreams. He traveled far and wide—from St. Petersburg to Paris and Berlin. And in every city, he told people about *Pictures at an Exhibition,* making sure that Victor lived forever in the music of Modest Mussorgsky.

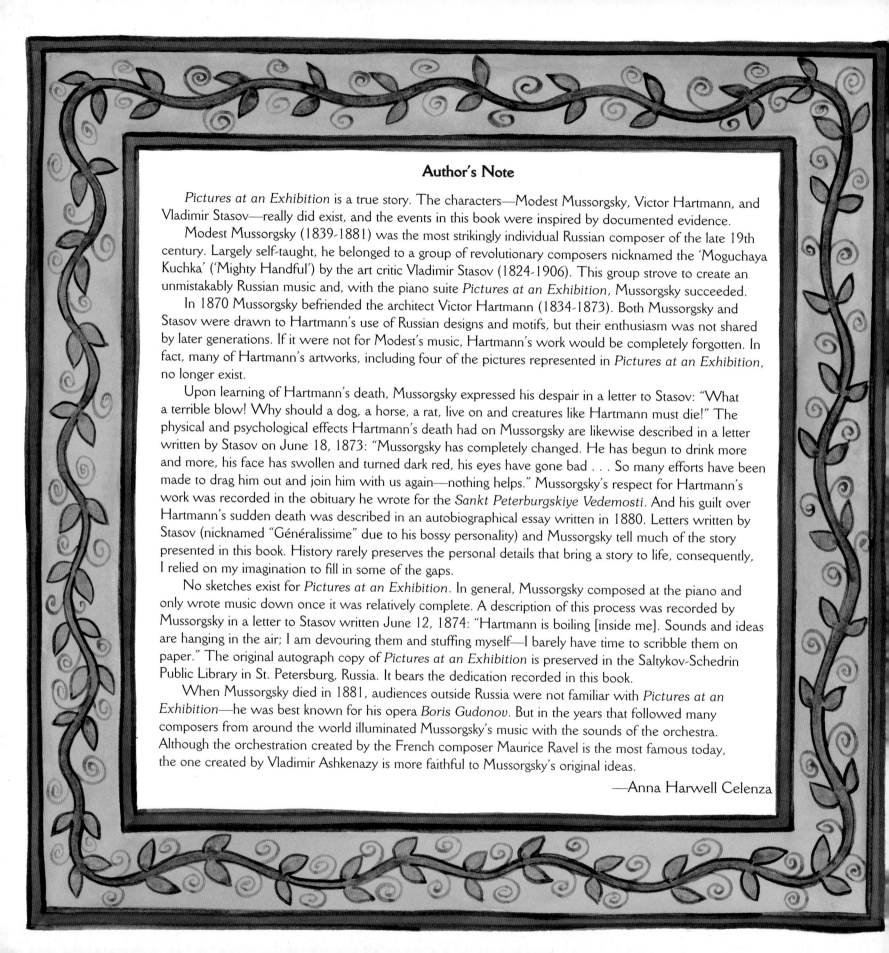

Author's Note

Pictures at an Exhibition is a true story. The characters—Modest Mussorgsky, Victor Hartmann, and Vladimir Stasov—really did exist, and the events in this book were inspired by documented evidence.

Modest Mussorgsky (1839-1881) was the most strikingly individual Russian composer of the late 19th century. Largely self-taught, he belonged to a group of revolutionary composers nicknamed the 'Moguchaya Kuchka' ('Mighty Handful') by the art critic Vladimir Stasov (1824-1906). This group strove to create an unmistakably Russian music and, with the piano suite *Pictures at an Exhibition*, Mussorgsky succeeded.

In 1870 Mussorgsky befriended the architect Victor Hartmann (1834-1873). Both Mussorgsky and Stasov were drawn to Hartmann's use of Russian designs and motifs, but their enthusiasm was not shared by later generations. If it were not for Modest's music, Hartmann's work would be completely forgotten. In fact, many of Hartmann's artworks, including four of the pictures represented in *Pictures at an Exhibition*, no longer exist.

Upon learning of Hartmann's death, Mussorgsky expressed his despair in a letter to Stasov: "What a terrible blow! Why should a dog, a horse, a rat, live on and creatures like Hartmann must die!" The physical and psychological effects Hartmann's death had on Mussorgsky are likewise described in a letter written by Stasov on June 18, 1873: "Mussorgsky has completely changed. He has begun to drink more and more, his face has swollen and turned dark red, his eyes have gone bad . . . So many efforts have been made to drag him out and join him with us again—nothing helps." Mussorgsky's respect for Hartmann's work was recorded in the obituary he wrote for the *Sankt Peterburgskiye Vedemosti*. And his guilt over Hartmann's sudden death was described in an autobiographical essay written in 1880. Letters written by Stasov (nicknamed "Généralissime" due to his bossy personality) and Mussorgsky tell much of the story presented in this book. History rarely preserves the personal details that bring a story to life, consequently, I relied on my imagination to fill in some of the gaps.

No sketches exist for *Pictures at an Exhibition*. In general, Mussorgsky composed at the piano and only wrote music down once it was relatively complete. A description of this process was recorded by Mussorgsky in a letter to Stasov written June 12, 1874: "Hartmann is boiling [inside me]. Sounds and ideas are hanging in the air; I am devouring them and stuffing myself—I barely have time to scribble them on paper." The original autograph copy of *Pictures at an Exhibition* is preserved in the Saltykov-Schedrin Public Library in St. Petersburg, Russia. It bears the dedication recorded in this book.

When Mussorgsky died in 1881, audiences outside Russia were not familiar with *Pictures at an Exhibition*—he was best known for his opera *Boris Gudonov*. But in the years that followed many composers from around the world illuminated Mussorgsky's music with the sounds of the orchestra. Although the orchestration created by the French composer Maurice Ravel is the most famous today, the one created by Vladimir Ashkenazy is more faithful to Mussorgsky's original ideas.

—Anna Harwell Celenza